The publication of *Five Kentucky Poets Laureate: An Anthology* is a project of the Kentucky Arts Council made possible through an American Masterpieces grant from the National Endowment for the Arts.

The Kentucky Arts Council is a state agency in the Tourism, Arts and Heritage Cabinet that provides opportunities for Kentuckians to value, participate in and benefit from the arts.

Kentucky Arts Council funding is provided by the Kentucky State Legislature and the National Endowment for the Arts, which believes that a great nation deserves great art.

PRINTED WITH STATE FUNDS

Library of Congress Control Number: 2008931657

Cover photograph, *Barn with Tree Limb*, by Geoff Carr

Five Kentucky Poets Laureate:

An Anthology

———————————

edited by

Jane Gentry

&

Frederick Smock

Table of Contents

Acknowledgments

Poems by Richard Taylor are drawn from a current manuscript of sonnets, *Rail-Splitter*, and the books *Brain Tree* (Scienter Press), *The Country of Morning Calm* (Larkspur Press), and *Stone Eye* (Larkspur Press).

James Baker Hall's story is an excerpt from a novel-in-manuscript about University of Kentucky basketball entitled *The Loving Nowhere*, which was first published in *Wind*, and is reprinted here with the permission of its editors, Erik Tuttle and Nick Smith.

Poems by Joe Survant are drawn from his collections *The Presence of Snow in the Tropics* (Landmark Books), *We Will All Be Changed* (State Street Press), and, from the University of Arkansas Press, *Anne & Alpheus 1842-1882* and *Rafting Rise*.

Sena Jeter Naslund's short story, "The Perfecting of the Chopin *Valse No. 14 in E Minor*," first appeared in *The Georgia Review*, and was reprinted in her story collection *Ice-Skating at the North Pole* (Ampersand Press).

Poems by Jane Gentry are quite new, and are only now seeking their way into the world.

Preface

"Kentucky is a writerly state," observed Jim Wayne Miller, himself a poet and long-time teacher at Western Kentucky University. Ever since Daniel Boone crossed through the Cumberland Gap into Kentucky, and wrote the first poem composed west of the Appalachians, on a tree – *D. Boon kilt a bar, 1803* – Kentuckians have been living the examined life.

The supreme achievement of Kentucky letters might well be read in the work of its poets laureate. The current volume publishes selections from the five living poets laureate, and the works are as varied as you might expect from a state that bridges east and west, north and south – the Mason-Dixon line ran down the middle of Market Street in Louisville, after all. Sena Jeter Naslund contributes a short story about two women – a mother and daughter – conjoined through art, as they contemplate a rather magical process of aging. Joe Survant's poems are polished to a spare elegance, yet contain a surfeit of emotion; he gives eloquent voice to frontier people, male and female. Richard Taylor's poems reflect his deep interest in local history and, as well, philosophy and the natural world. Though known primarily as a poet, James Baker Hall – ever unpredictable – contributes a short story about U.K. basketball, perhaps the greatest passion in all of the Bluegrass State. And, Jane Gentry's poems speak in exquisite language about that double-headed coin, joy/loss, or to shift the metaphor, the two poles of experience upon which our world tilts and turns.

As you read, you will perhaps also notice some similarities running under the surface variety. Such is the universal and variable nature of life and art.

Frederick Smock

Introduction

The Kentucky Arts Council is pleased to present this volume of writing by Kentucky Poets Laureate. Their commitment to telling their stories follows the strong literary heritage of the commonwealth, where Kentuckians have long put pen to paper to record their thoughts, observations and dreams.

The position of Kentucky Poet Laureate was originally established in 1926 by an act of the Kentucky General Assembly. Prior to 1990, Kentucky Poets Laureate were appointed to lifetime terms by the General Assembly and at times several people held the position simultaneously. In 1990, new legislation was enacted to provide for the gubernatorial appointment of the state Poet Laureate. Appointed for two-year terms to honor the commonwealth's strong literary tradition and promote the literary arts, Kentucky's Poets Laureate must reside in Kentucky, have a long association with the commonwealth, and have a critically acclaimed published body of work that is informed by living in Kentucky. The public call for nominations is coordinated by the Kentucky Arts Council.

The Poets Laureate have each spent their two-year term traveling across the commonwealth to celebrate and promote the literary arts through readings, workshops, meeting with students, educators and writers, participating in Kentucky Writers Day, and serving as literary consultants to the Kentucky Arts Council.

Our thanks to Jane Gentry, Sena Jeter Naslund, Joe Survant, James Baker Hall, and Richard Taylor for sharing their stories with us.

Lori Meadows
Executive Director
Kentucky Arts Council
Summer 2008

Richard Taylor

Young Lincoln in a Moment of Revelation

His finger inches along the furrows of print, dirt
of southern Indians crusted under the nail.
At the end of each row, he presses to the next,
the turkeyfeet miraculously shaping letters,
sweet bundles of gist. As the chimney's updraft
wavers his light, the words tremble suddenly
into sense, take on sounds his voice can fit
to a Kentucky accent. By "littles" he learns—
from Weems's *Washington*, from King James,
from Crusoe tracking across a deserted shore,
from a bard whose plantings root in his loam,
recasting a wilderness of gray bark into orchards:
"better angels of our nature," "a house divided…,"
"four score & seven years," "malice toward none."

Lincoln's Photographer, Alexander Gardner

Eyeing his unforgiving portraits of Lincoln
toward war's end calls up Ambrose Bierce's
entry for photography in *The Devil's Dictionary*,
"A picture painted by the sun without instruction
in art." Though guilty at Antietam of propping
a dead sniper in his den to dramatize at least
one narrative in light, Gardner caught Lincoln's
most un-self-conscious self—his grainy cheeks,
a weary resilience in one glinting eye, a caving
slope of shoulder defined by the shadow's heft—
going on to shoot (after his subject's complete
merger into darkness) a first photo sequence of
history-as-it-happened as four conspirators hanged:
Mary Surratt dropping, her hooded head a blur.

15   *Richard Taylor*

Frederick Douglass

In him Lincoln saw his replica in black,
parallel lives in poorness, self-tutoring,
a rise to eminence by will and locomotion.
"This is not time," ran Douglass's argument
for black enlistment, "to fight with one hand,"
his homey metaphors hitting home. "A man
drowning would not refuse to be saved even
by a colored hand." When Lincoln welcomed
him after his "malice toward none" inaugural
as though he were not the White House's
first black guest, Douglass declared the speech
"a sacred effort." It made his "heart jump."
Lincoln gave this caulker of ships his favorite
walking stick, "not to a color but to a man."

Triumph

Barging on the James with as little stir as Sunday
outings before the war, Lincoln entered Richmond.
Blacks along the rubbled streets shouted messiah,
called him Father Abraham, some kneeling as if
to kiss feet. Curiosity drove him to his rival's
White House where that other Kentuckian worked
and fretted—floor strewn with maps and papers
but shelves of books, unlike their owner's armies,
still standing in even rows. Seated in the chair
in which Jeff Davis sat (imagining it still warm),
Lincoln savored seeing the world as that man
saw it—same walls, same window light, arm rails
oiled by a stranger's hands. Saying, "Thank God
I've lived to see this." Then ten days later, dead.

Mary in Mourning

Though war at times bore Lincoln down so hard
it seemed his "mind had left its throne," it was
Mary's mother-love that took her to the edge
& sometimes over, upheld by faith that she could
summon sons Willie, Eddie, from the spirit world.
Giving up on séance, deciding she herself could
lift the veils between the realms, she insisted Willie
stood nightly smiling at her bed's foot, sometimes
even little Eddie. Her life was bordered, like her
writing papers, with a band of black, night's color
that tokened her withdrawal from the world
of martial bands and laughter. Even the jewels
she wore were black. She lived encircled by great
clouds of spirits hovering denser than Antietam.

Cattle Song

Nathan Banks, a 22-year-old student at Purchase
College, painted single words on the flanks of about
60 cows near his upstate New York home, then let
them wander around to see if they could compose
poetry.
  — Associated Press

Outside my window I see lettered angus
on the hillside composing pastorals,
cantos to clover, a haiku whose theme
this July morning is sweet surrender
to the dark cove of an encompassing oak,
a deep draught of rainwater in a silver tank.

From my own skirmishes with words,
I know, odds are, most tries will fail.
The calf will stand on wobbly legs.
The field of sweet grass stiffens into frost.
One moo will echo every other moo.

Richard Taylor

Still, watching, I imagine a taut-uddered
genius, a Holstein Homer maybe,
a moony Sappho whose words take
on life down some trackless cowpath
the reader never dares to wander.

Now, as the grazers bunch, break off, and roam,
I try to sequence them into sense, to herd
them whole like some dismantled sonnet,
a fragmented script of some language lost
that they, that we, will never understand.

Writing Slump

As I drive to work, the sky is void
as though the clouds have seceded
to compose their own republic of rain.

The red fox that scurried across
the road last week, the one I'd been saving
for a poem, insists she's only a red fox.

Even the puddles from yesterday's shower,
metallic and flat as spatulas, shrug off
light and hold the shadows hostage.

I imagine my son's stolen Honda
being dismantled in some chop shop,
an automotive diaspora-its disc player

surgically transplanted, radials married
to a pickup, say, in Alabama, hub caps
migrating to some Valhalla of chrome.

Something will come, I tell myself.
Still, the mimosa holds its tongue
it's pucker-pink blossoms speechless.

In an act of unwitting collaboration
that describes her state and mine,
my mother calls to say, "Some days
I feel I'm fading into Bolivia."

Impedagogy

Experts tell us that only thirty percent
of any class at any time is actually listening.

During an exposition of Nietzsche's slave morality
or the intricacies of the comma splice, students

fantasize about pepperoni and extra mozzarella,
someone's cleavage two desks down,

the next episode of *The Young and the Restless*.
Towards fall and spring breaks, reception flags,

like the ailing radio in my son's geriatric Honda,
always on but only sometimes receiving,

cutting off or on each time we hit a bump.
Opening and slamming the driver's door,

I can revive the stray signals, the fragile contact,
as sound waves bustle in the corridor of air.

Restoring reception in class is not so certain
as I jar the dozers with direct address,

transmit thunder by means of the augering eye.
Compared, the car-door by far is more reliable.

Richard Taylor

Sizing My Ecological Footprint

Lime is how I paint myself, moderately
green, before unearthing a website
that gauges my impact on the planet.

Putting my best foot forward, I cite
recycling sports pages by the bale,
bandoleers of Bud Lites, scalloped

plastic trays of microwave dinners.
If my windows lack double panes,
I compensate with thermowear,

my furnace never topping a summit
of sixty lean degrees. I gloat
when data inform my office mate

that if all of us imitated his sleek
suburban life, we would need
a boost of 9.3 additional earths.

Then I weigh in at 7.5, reminded
of my faulty septic field,
my clunker coughing up its oily spew,

my children three, some guilty shares
of Global Oil, lapsed Sierra dues—
an ecological footprint not so deep as wide,

like say, a tarred Nike with gripper treads,
not hooves that mangle as they strut but blend
in tainted paths with anyone's, with yours.

One Fine Day at September's End

The neighbor I greet at Kroger's
with what a beautiful day it is
says, "Yeah, good for fishing,"
angling his ladened cart toward checkout.

Though I don't fish, I feel the lure
that pulls him, imagining the sun
that splays across the pool
on Elkhorn Creek, ample, umber,
in perfect balance with the ragged hem
of blue shadow along its banks.

Then I remember the e-mail
I must wade through at the office:
the group excuse for student athletes,
a cheery reminder that the handbook
committee will meet at eleven,
a frittata of flavorless memos
that will not unscramble into sense,
their vagueness abundantly vaguer
than the terrace of riffles downstream
scored with silver furrows.

At the meeting, sinking in my seat,
I can almost sense sunlight
on my cheek. As the agenda hovers,
I ponder the endless variations
in constancy by which water
weaves and unweaves itself,
O sweet Penelope!,
the flow of current over stones,
the algae hugging those stones—

opening, reading *that* mail.

Richard Taylor

In Praise of Sycamores
For David Orr (1942-1989)

Mention that tree around here
and you summon up Paul Sawyier,
our local impressionist
whose creekscapes blaze with sycamores,
gaudy lemons and ochers
that burn in some eternal summer,
their broad leaves shimmering
above the placid nooks
of some angler's dream.

Cross-grained, unsplittable,
their wood makes butchers' blocks
and not much else
beyond nourishment for the eye—
a blue heaven for the artist.
Lugging only his paint kit, bedroll,
and a tin of nightcrawlers,
Sawyier vanished for days up Elkhorn Creek
to commit his gentle arsons,
constellations of briars starring
the worsteds above his scruffy boots.

Each sycamore is the product of place.
Elbowed by neighbors along the creek,
its crown is vase-shaped, almost modest,
its stem as columnar as swans.

But on open ground it spreads
in pearly tiers like antlers,
its twists and goose-necked spirals
elegant as candelabra,
the trophy of some buried stag.
Winter's tree,

its bark is winter's flag,
an utterance of ice.

Unlike the cedar,
its architecture does not tame itself
to models, will not repeat.
Answering only to persuasions
of rainfall and light,
of soil and creekside rivals,
it persists
as a miscellany of upthrust limbs
whose scoured bark,
gleaming brilliantly white
against the somber hills,
has tracings as precise and eloquent
as veins on the anatomist's chart,
an embroidery that stitch for stitch
knits up the creek
with filigree and frill
to lend the valleys hereabout
some luster, some civility.

The Lava Beds at Pompeii

Using a steel rod, Guiseppe Fiorelli
first tapped the crust in 1863,
finding hollows where humans
had dried up and all but vanished.
In these pockets he poked holes,
filling the curious voids with plaster.

When it set, he pried out
a plaster man, suffocating,
clawing at his underclothes,
then another clutching coins.
Next, a woman hugging a child,

Richard Taylor

two gladiators doomed in their cells
still manacled to the wall,
even a dog straining at it's leash.

What they hold in common
is August 24, 79 A.D., a day
when morning went night
and rained pumice, rivers
of volcanic ash flowing down
the Via dell' Abbondanze
to smother it under twenty feet
of sulphuric silt.

Street by street, yard by yard,
Fiorelli reclaimed what he could:
black loaves from the baker's oven,
a cup unfinished on the potter's wheel,
a table set for noon.

Now, after two millennia,
the victims plead through museum glass,
still writhe against extinction,
affirming all that is human
in the tension of an upraised hand,
a gaping mouth—
agonies more eloquent than speech.

On Whapping My
Index Finger with
a Roofing Hammer

This time it happens on the garage
nailing shingles, driving
steel on steel through asphalt, felt,
and poplar sheathing tacked down
before McKinley was shot.

Spring is still a murmur,
the yard simmering with patches
of scrawny green, wands
in the water maples
blushing lavender
against the sober ridge.

From his pickup window
Jim Haney waves, yells up
to ask if I'm doing any good-
just enough distraction
to skew the dropping hammer,
his wife and teenage daughter
wincing in the cab
when I shout the most basic verb
that pain can summon.

Yowling, offending the righteous—
imprecision has other costs.
Add the cuticle's shattered moon,
the blue-black scarab
already trapped beneath the nail.
This throbbing cannot match
even one forsythia
whose swollen buds muscle just now
their yellow liberation into bloom.

Richard Taylor

Severn Creek
— for Gray Zeitz of Larkspur

For the third spring we trek
the disused country road,
deer prints pressing ground
made soft by yesterday's showers.
In gray tiers, hardwoods rise up
toward the cedared bluffs.
The luscious glut of creekwater
riffles through us intimate as breath.

It's early. Spring purrs its lime
among the branchtips—not yet
an exclamation. The trout lily
has performed its bloom,
but the Dutchman's-breeches
are still furled like silken flags.
Fire pinks still smolder
hours shy of floral combustion,
the beds of bluebells
we hiked miles to see
already basking in the bottoms.

As we pass a bank of larkspurs,
each spiked floret asserting
its purple integrity, its tensile grace,
Gray, inspired, declares this occasion
the annual meeting of his board.

With a simple show of hands
the membership, each sprig, each
spacious leaf, reaffirms its policy
to vegetate the hills,
following by-laws to the letter
with each corporate tendril,
each dash of color, as we all assent
to raise, to resurrect, the dead.

The Abolitionist Cassius Clay Steps Briefly Out of His Memoirs During a Severe Drought

Under this cobalt sky
that holds not one rumor,
one smudge of moisture,
the 'Lion of White Hall' revives.
Not the duelist, soldier, diplomat,
but his wavery shadow,
an old man in his eighties armed
with only a small brass cannon
against the twin demons
of loneliness and despair.

Twice divorced, shunned
by his surviving children,
sequestered in an empty house—
a thirty-room fortress in which
he nurses his parched spirit.
He makes the best of exile,
his beard and uncut hair graying
'with the frost which never melts.'

During the day he keeps society
with flowers and shrubs.
He gathers about him 'dogs
and pigeons and barnfowls'—
even the 'mute fishes.'
A bird cage hangs from the sweetgum
under which he reads Plutarch
or Stowe, a crumb-box
nailed to the window ledge.

Each night he swings open
his bedroom shutters
to draw in the bats, consoled,

Richard Taylor

exhilarated, as they flit about
snatching flies from the wall plaster.
His greatest pleasure, their fluttering
wingbeats, 'life, life!'

Dreaming the Buffalo Back

In droves their swollen humps
rise from the shallows, hooves
nicking the asphalt with tiny moons.

Tracking the scent of salt,
they graze resolutely east,
past patios, through fences
and staked tomatoes
toward Stamping Ground,
the bowl-shaped wallow
where they will hunker and swill.

Muzzle to tail, they migrate.
To Sulphur Lick and Great Crossing,
to all places that carry
their lost names. Shaggy pilgrims,
bearded, robed in snow,
they bunch at night
to blanket their quaking calves.

Under a spatterwork of stars
they herd in the lush pasturage
of dream. Without predators,
they reclaim the landscape
encompassed between the parentheses
of their upturned horns.
Loosed from memory,
they cannot even dream
the space where we might be.

Along the Bluegrass Parkway
In Early Spring

Lulled as the hills slide by,
my eye follows the stripe
of torch-shaped cedars
that jag along the embankment
mile after mile after mile.

Each forms a shaggy cone
with bristles that rise
dark as the undersides
of waves, tactile as fur.

Then, prying between the bushy
crowns, redbuds spray into view.
Against the dingy conifers,
the pallid slopes, they detonate
in geysers of light, petals liquid
and pink as a calf's tongue.

Long after the landscape flattens,
they hover in the mind:
pink fretwork lit in bright
swatches, pushy branchlets
reared by fluxions of light
and native inclination.

Richard Taylor

First Monday on Sabbatical

For nearly an hour this morning,
I listen to the steady rain
as it beats along the eaves
and patters to the walk
in detonations small, irregular,
that language has no word for.

These lavish seepings that
soak the tree hydrangea to its roots,
that ping the bucket blue,
free us from the human drive
to measure things, to fit
the rhythms of this world to rhyme.

These plashes, this seething vibrato,
shape the morning
only in their constancy:
wordless, tactile, wetly random.

James Baker Hall

from *The Loving Nowhere*

You can study all the old pictures, the stills and the films, and you can study all the line scores with a good memory for details no one else notices, you can know all the year-end won-lost records, and the post-season records, and who was on which team, and how tall they were and where they came from, six-foot-five-inch Lou Tsipropolus out of Lynn, Massachusetts (when six-five was tall and weight lifting was strictly for body-builders, something those old pictures of mid-century players will keep reminding you of), and who King Rex played his first game against as a Cat (Austin Peay), and how many he garnered in scorching Louisville in his freshman year (twenty-whoa-six), and how many in his sophomore year in his last game as a Cat (thirty, Villanova, NCAA) —

You can know what happened to most of the memorable players and a few not so memorable after they graduated, and you can know the coaches and their staffs like an American historian knows the U.S. Presidents and their cabinets, and how many children each head coach and each assistant had and whether or not they were ballplayers, and if so, how good. The Pitino kids, for instance, ball-boys at the pre-game warm-ups, towel-wielding chair-boys during the action, wiping up sweat and clearing off bad-call shit thrown onto the floor, who returned to the locker room for final instruction before the tunnel-funnel count-down to tip-off, and again at half-time after the half-time show was over, displaying their skills before the milling full-house at famous Rupp, with some watching with binocs and evaluating and conversing with those around them in section 215 row JJ seats 24, 25 and 26. *Where do those kids go to school,* someone asked, *Sayre, I'll bet,* someone answered. *No,* a pre-teen said, *they go to Lexington Catholic,* and someone else said, *Is Pitino a Catholic,* and Buford said, *He's got a New England priest in his entourage,* and the pre-teen said, *He's got five children,* and her father said, *Five boys,* and somebody else said, *No, one's a girl, I'm pretty sure,* and Buford said, *They also lost a child,* and the pre-teen said, *One's a girl,* to somebody on the other side who hadn't heard her father — as the youngest Pitino down there on the shiny floor launched his first Rupp Arena public three on a brother-dare, which looked more like a pass to one of them waiting under the basket (as long as you didn't have to decide which one), to scattered amusement among those who would applaud next season when the youngster scored his first Rupp three, and as Buford took his binocs back from the Larkspur Press Buddha-mon Zietz behind them, he said, *I'd love to watch what must go on at school between those kids and their teammates,* and Buddha-mon, smiling at Laci, who was too young to join the banter, said, *Me too,* and his friend Leslie said, *Me too,* and his handsome brother-in-law Bill several seats farther away, with his smiling, reddish-blond wife between, took off his radio head-set to hear what they were saying -

You could know who was the first Cat to average twenty points a game (Alex Groza), and how long the record held (sixteen years) and who broke it (Cotton Nash), and who was the all time UK leading scorer (Dan Issel), and the various basketball jobs he held in his afterlife, and you could know in order all the members of the career one-thousand point club, and which ones played fewer than four years, and all the members of the five-hundred rebound club and the two-hundred assist club, and you could know more than anybody else about Pat Riley's off-court life, and who Linville Puckett's high school teammates were, and who he married and who she dated at Henry Clay High School before she married him (Buford's daddy), and what made the sarcastic Rupp ride Linville, especially, with Sarcasm, and what made Linville say what he did to the Baron and walk off, and you could take special pride in the players from in state and know their wives' maiden names and where the ceremony took place and who was in the wedding party and how long they'd gone together when they got married and how many of his teammates were in attendance, and be disappointed and a little disoriented if at least one or two weren't in the wedding party —

You could know that Fabulous Fiver Cliff Barker, a twenty-three-year-old WWII vet who could make the ball do anything but talk, was the first Cat ever to dribble behind his

James Baker Hall

back in a game (out-of-town for sure, probably Madison Square Garden), and that the Baron Adolph, who was still making his players shoot free-throws under-handed, jumped out of his already-famous brown suit and benched Barker and as the story goes wouldn't speak even Sarcasm to him after the game or admit to those up-East sportswriters that he'd seen any such foolishness from one of his boys, and know that the play nonetheless entered Wildcat history via the game film (made by Buford's daddy), and was so strange to fans of the late forties that they had a hard time seeing it even after being alerted —

You could know that the Baron Adolph occasioned many a good laugh that goes on and on entertaining the Faithful, like when he said that up-East game-fixing racketeers couldn't touch his good Southern boys with a ten-foot pole shortly before the first wave of point-shaving arrests hit UK and the House of Champions trophy cases had to be opened up and purged of all traces of UK's association with certain of its most celebrated heroes —

You could know which teams suffered from NCAA sanctions in what way, and that the Hagan-Ramsey teams of the early fifties, barred from post-season play, could have won UK three more national championships, and that the student manager on that team, Humzey Yes sir, was a starter on the baseball team (was it at second or short?), and know that Humzey had a sister named Hilda who worked in the alumni office on the second floor of what was then the Student Center and is now the Old Student Center, and that Cliff took her out a couple of times, an unlikely couple because he was a 6'4" look-oh-look Greek god, and she was on the short and dumpy side, like her brother, and not a beauty —

You can know what Governor A.B. "Happy" Chandler said to Adoph Rupp at halftime of the last game in Memorial Coliseum, and what Rupp said to Happy after he sang "My Old Kentucky Home" at the end of the game, and what Joanne Pitino was supposed to have *really* felt about Lexington, and who that was sitting with Tubby's wife Donna for this game and that and another, a staple of binoc life in Rupp, and how many games UK Kappa Kappa Gamma Ashley Judd came to in 2002, and in what order the president of the University and his wife and the Governor and his wife lined up to visit her in her seat in the student sixth-man E-*Rupp*-tion Zone before the tip-off of whatever game that was, and know which year it was Ashley skipped the Academy Awards to be there for her team ("The Academy Awards is just entertainment, UK basketball is life."), and which year it was the bag-checkers were replaced by metal-detectors, and how long after that before the first National Guard troops started showing up at games in unit formations, and asserting their presence, with assault weapons and gas masks, from roof tops all over the neighborhood, and how many parking-lot and curb-side vehicles were destroyed during the Louisville game on the night the IED record was set -

You can even know what it's like to drive into Lexington on game day past Bluegrass Field and see all the private jets from around the state and around the region and a few regulars from afar, Dallas, Saratoga, Fort Lauderdale, Fort Myers, Cleveland, parked wingtip to wingtip in an area used also by the National Guard, the fan crews in the Hyatt bar downtown, or bellied-up across the street at deSha's, ready to go back to work after the game or lay-over however long, and know some of the highrollers involved who kept apartments at the Hanover Towers or nearer-to-Rupp at the Park Plaza and nearer still, at the 500s on West Main, and know which ones came to town how often during the (usually) downer football season —

And know at what time the Faithful coming by car leave Morehead ninety miles away passing tobacco barn after tobacco farm after cow barn with hoops nailed over sliding doors, two-story frame houses from the nineteenth century with a hoop and backboard out back, small towns with netless hoops and backboards and ill-kempt courts in the park, with backboards and netless hoops nailed onto telephone poles, with plastic mobile kiddie hoops in the drive in three sizes and/or nerf-hoops in the open garage, mobile homes with concrete-block steps and weeds growing over the windows with a hoop nailed up somewhere, and the only grass control in a semi-circle around it. Or from

Louisville eighty miles away passing subdivisions, and know when you saw a house without a basketball goal in evidence, you were looking at the way people live without children or grandchildren or friends (unless there's a six-footer in the basement) —

Buford was partial to the helicopter view himself, watching the Faithful with their K flags flying converge from all over the state with hours to spare, with pre-game rituals to attend to, a loner from way down in Inez, several from far-off Paducah, three from Whitesburg traveling in tandem, several from Bowling Green and then several more, and scores from Louisville, until the Faithful were backing out of the garage each on schedule and turning toward Lexington from every part of the state, catching wind in the blue flying white Ks, Danville, Frankfort, Monterey, Mount Sterling, Owensboro, Middlesboro, Cynthiana, and soon enough laced-in National Guard vehicles on duty, one unit from Jefferson County, another from Leslie County, troop carriers led by a Jeep with its lights flashing. With an hour or two to spare before tipoff the fans commenced noticing each other and tooting and waving and yelling GO CATS, mostly SUV's with blue and white Wildcat flags mounted atop the back doors. Ten miles outside Lexington and increasing as they came in 1-64 and 1-75 and the Bluegrass Parkway and the Mountain Parkway and the Versailles Pike and the Newtown Pike and the Winchester Pike, you saw the season-ticket Faithful punctuated by the combat-ready gathering together like spokes on a moving wheel, like tank fish at feed time, and once they were off the arterials they bunched like minnows in one and another of the funnels into Rupp —

Most of them would be listening to the radio before-game coverage, which started commentary and call-ins two hours before the tip, and would be listening to it all the way home, to the after-game stats and commentary and interviews and summaries before the serious stuff started when the lines were declared open and the calls started coming in, Billy from Hazard, *Okay, Billy from Hazard, you're on,* and Billy said, *How you guys doing,* and one of them said, *Doing good, doing good,* and the other one said, *Doing better than good after that game. What's on your mind, Billy from Hazard. Did you approve of the play of our boy Lights Out Lukens tonight,* and Billy said, *Well, I didn't understand why J. C. took him out with eight minutes to play,* and talk-show one said, *UK was forty-two points ahead,* and Billy said, *You got a point,* and talk-show two said, It's my humble opinion that you got to give those guys who show up for practice every day a chance to get in a game every now and then,* and Billy said, *You got a point,* and talk-show one said, *What if he got hurt in the last eight minutes and we were up forty-two? You wouldn't be able to understand why J.C. left him in,* and Billy said, *You got a point,* and talk-show two said, *One more thing, Billy. Then we've got to give Mike in Bowling Green a chance,* and Billy said, *When you go hunting, you want to see your dog hunt,* and talk-show one said, *I'm on your side, Billy. Here's a question for you. Is the boy as good as the hype?* and Billy said, *I'd like to* *see him pass more. When he gets into the N.B.A., he's going to have to pass the ball,* and talk-show one said, *You know, Billy, he had nineteen assists tonight,* and Billy said, *You got a point,* and talk-show two said, *Billy from Hazard, thanks for calling, have a good one!*

And know how long the food lines in the food court were an hour and a half before the tip, an hour fifteen, an hour, and know how it translated into lost time for the shoot-around, as compared to hot dogs, a coke and popcorn purchased inside by someone who knew where the short lines were, the dogs fixed in mustard and relish at the condiment shelf way over yonder with a touch of catsup and wrapped in napkins (because the foil sleeves took two hands to reenter, and a patience hard to sustain in such a press of people), and eaten in view of the team coming out the tunnel for the first shoot-around, all the house lights still on, and the first units of the smartly camouflaged National Guard appearing in formation, then breaking down into threes and fives to begin their patrols —

You could know what it was like to have to hunt for a seat in the blue-and-white food court and hunt and hunt some more, separated from your companions for double or triple coverage, and no matter where you might end up seated, with grandparents from Ashland bringing their grandson to his first game, all three of them dressed alike in blue and white sweats, with gran wearing blue flashing-lights earrings, or a scholarly father and his Harry Potter son from nearby Midway — know

James Baker Hall

that conversation would be welcome and spirited —

Who's your favorite player? kid Laci asked the five-year-old boy with his grandparents, years before the question was a Joke in the Year of LO.

Ke-Iennn-naa A<u>zzz</u>-i-buuu-kie, the kid nailed it, imitating the Rupp Arena announcer's voice. —-

Mine too! the youngster Sunny Boone said, standing up to reach over there and high-five the kid and then, moving fast with both hands, high-fived Laci then Buford then grandpaw and grandmaw. *He looks like Tarzan and he doesn't play like Jane!,* which was a take-off on something Tubby had said. —

Or what it was like in the Hyatt lobby an hour and a half before tip when it was Louisville as compared to Pitt, and how it changed as the countdown continued, know throughout your whole body the heart value of the ticket you held, and the forlorn vibe of those cruising about holding up two fingers, and know in detail how the local and state police deal with each other and with the hotel security personnel and the patrolling guardsmen, and who the seven-footer was kissing the lady Cats coach Micky DeMoss on top of the head, and which old players could be expected to make an appearance in the big open pit of the bar just off the lobby, Anthony Epps for instance, and wonder who those people were coming up to him for handshakes and hugs and cheek kisses —

You could know personally people who've had their

42

wedding date changed after the announcements were sent out when someone noticed that there was a game that day, and someone who couldn't get legally divorced because no agreement was possible concerning the season tickets, and someone else who'd paid thousands of dollars to be buried in a blue and white plastic coffin, and somebody else with UK inscribed on the white of his glass eyeball, and somebody else ready and proud to go to jail for roughing-up a referee who'd made one-too-many bad calls in Rupp (that was Buford, years before the boy), and someone else who refused an offer of fifteen grand for three upper arena tickets in the Year of LO, that was Buford also, whose girls no longer accompanied him (Sunny Boone had a press pass, Laci was home with the baby) and who could himself enter Rupp with the team and sit on the bench whenever he wanted to, but wasn't about to forego the company he got to keep on the next-to-last row up, where the Faithful lived up to their responsibilities (unlike too many in the lower arena who thought that the game began with the tip and throughout sat silently on their money-fat asses and left early, if they hadn't handed their tickets off to friends or kin) —

You could know the stir that passed throughout the crowd of twenty-four thousand plus when the house lights started down, and the big screens throughout the arena quit showing tapes and went live to the tunnel to show the team out of the dressing room now: bunching up and bouncing on the balls of their feet and dancing around and waiting for the signal, and the growing stir when more and more people took up watching the screens and the house lights went down another notch and the scatter of noise quit scattering and quieted down in anticipation, fathers pointing their small children where to watch, taking them up in arms, until everyone's attention was on what was going on via high-def tv in the tunnel, the one with the towel on his head, the one with the towel on his head —

You could know your endless Wildcat stuff, and still have no idea what it was like to be down there in that tunnel funnel with the team and the tv cameras and the camouflaged soldiers waiting for the signal that it's time to take the floor and play the game: the four assistant coaches, the four student managers, the trainers, the team doctor, twelve players suited up, three others not: the starters stripped now of their sweats, gathered to pyramid power each with an arm raised trying to touch hands at the top, **OH WHO'S IN THE HOUSE TONIGHT, OH WHO'S IN THE HOUSE TONIGHT,** they chant in the acoustical tunnel as they jump into each other trying to touch on high, **UK UK,** they hammer the reply into place: high energy getting off on itself and moving higher, aware that the pulsing crowd awaiting them out there in the dark is watching on in-house tv, that millions are watching over network tv, and listening as they chant **OH WHO'S IN THE HOUSE TONIGHT** one last time, and **UK** one last time: as they split off and surge out of the tunnel and down the funnel chute led by the smallest player toward the waiting cheerleaders who precede them with jumps, cartwheels, cheers, waving arms, flips and spins into the spotlights: which pick them up as soon as they appear and follow them out onto the floor live, flanked by armed troops, as the fans turn up the volume, themselves aware that millions across the country and the sports world world-wide are watching not just their team but them, the much talked-about Big Blue Faithful: proving that they are worthy to host the hyped-out debut of the most hyped-out eighteen-year-old athlete in U.S. hyped-out sports history, at Rupp in Lexington, the perfect setting —

Set 'em up, the boy is hungry, everybody is hungry.

When the team flowed in a trotting line out of the tunnel into the spotlights and went through a final three circles of layups, everybody watched number 8 ease through this ritual with the rest of them, passing twice and shooting twice, not showing anybody anything they wanted to see, while half of the seventeen-out-of-the-last-eighteen-years-national-championship cheerleaders commenced their four-beat C-A-T-S chant, dividing the crowd up north east south and west and getting each to compete with the others, the thermometer-shaped noise-meter visible on the in-house screens, and the other half did back-flips up and down the middle of the floor now that the teams had retired to their benches, and the tv folks gave the signal for the serious wind-up to commence.

James Baker Hall

The ROTC honor guard presented the colors, and Everett McCorvey, the faculty star of stars of UK's renowned music school, sang the National Anthem. When the house lights went out, the threes and fives quit patrolling but stayed vigilant as the three monster spot lights positioned on high went into their rhythmical, elliptical figure-eight trips around the darkened arena, slow at first, crisscrossing, bumping each other up and over and under, expanding coverage, and then picking up speed and fluidity as the organ entered into the build-up and took control, as the crowd started its rhythmical clapping, as the anticipation built, as the screens all over the throbbing house looped the excitement back into itself, as the organ went into its final approach to its final crescendo, which peaked and then peaked again with the rhythmical clapping and then ended, the house lights came back on, the troops resumed patrolling, and the announcer's voice boomed over the public address system: *Ladies and gentlemen, welcome to Rupp Arena, and tonight's basss-kettt-balll action, pitting the Tar Heels from the University of North Car-o-lina, against your University of Kentucky Willlddd-cats. And now for the starting line-ups. First, for North Carolina ...* One after the other the seated starters came off the cleared bench and walked, ambled, shuffled or skipped down the aisle created by their teammates, palm-slapping along the way, the last, to scattered boos, UNC's All-America power forward, and college basketball's Defensive Player of the Year, Barbarsweet

Zee, one of the four or five college players the pundits have been waiting to see the boy Lukens come up against. Finally the UNC coach was introduced, and the houselights went back off, the spotlights resumed their figure eights, grooved, precise, quick with anticipation, the organ made a brief reappearance, the crowd buzzed and began to resume shape. *Ladies and gentlemen, may I have your attention. Before the starting lineup for your University of Kentucky Willlldddd-cats, would you please direct your attention to overhead screens for the introduction of the honorary captains for tonight's game. First, out of Male High School in Louisville, Kentucky, a member of Adolph Rupp 's Fabulous Five, one of the greatest teams ever to play the game, an All-America in 1947, 1948 and 1949, an Olympic Gold Medal winner in 1948, one of the greatest players ever to play the game ... Ralph Beard!* The screen showed him in gum-chewing ball-stealing action first, and second in his last public appearance not all that many years before on that very floor, being introduced at the half time of the Louisville game, the spotlights following the aged but still nimble and as-of-that-night completely-forgiven completely-reintegrated Beard to the center of the court where he answered the crowd's roars with a lifted hand, pausing at the points of the compass, a tearful smile seen live throughout the arena on the hi-def screens, and rerun to open the Year of LO. *And next, from Owensboro, Kentucky, a member of the last undefeated Wildcat team in 1952, an All-America in 1950, 1951 and 1953, an NBA*

James Baker Hall

All Star with the St. Louis Hawks, the man many believe had the greatest hookshot the game has ever seen, off both wings ... Cliff Hagan! The overhead screen showed Hagan in swooping hook-shot action, followed by clips from his last public appearance likewise not all that many years ago on that very floor. In his late seventies at least, maybe early eighties, Hagan had looked fifty, and coming into the spotlights and into the standing ovation moved the way he always had, like honey coming over the lip of the jar. *And next, from Harlan, Kentucky, one of the most beloved personalities in the University of Kentucky legendary basketball history, the voice of the Cats from* 1954 *through* 1992, *we can't see him here with us tonight, but we know that he is here, and we can hear him* (with the word *voice,* the crowd fell immediately silent, the three spot lights separated and lined up in ellipsis from baseline to baseline) ... *Cawood Ledford.* The overhead screen pictured Cawood at the mike interviewing Coach Rupp, while over the p.a. came the announcer's voice, the Aesop to all the myths, calling selected moments of the 1978 NCAA championship game against Duke. *"Givens goes inside to Roby, who's double-teamed, back out to Macy, back over to Givens, who splits the double-team, gets off a jumper from fifteen, it's there, the Cats up by eight. The Goose is loose for the Wildcats ... the University of Kentucky has won its fifth national title tonight, on the back of a forty-one point performance by Jack 'Goose' Givens that will go down as one of the greatest the game has ever seen"*—

A slight pause allowed the gathering to return to the moment at hand, the organ piped back in, the spotlights resumed their rhythmical figure-eighting, they picked up speed, the in-house crowd quieted, in sports bars and theaters and gathering places around the world the crowds grew still as one after the other the lights zeroed in on the Kentucky bench that was cleared now except for the seated starters, one with a towel over his head, the camouflaged legs of three soldiers at parade rest in the spill light, gas masks hanging from their belts. *And now, the starting line-up for your University of Kentucky Willlldddd-cats!* As each of the starters was called forth, he came into the tube of lined-up reserves in a moving crouch, Ali Ali Akbar first, so that he could take and give low fives on both sides, and each shoulder-bumped or back-bumped those preceding and turned to join the rhythmical clapping that had been increasing in volume and intensity since the introductions began, and which now after the first four required the announcer to kick it up a notch to be heard. *And at forward, from Lexington, Kentucky, wearing jersey number 8 — he's not the reason we're here, ladies and gentlemen, but he's what we've all come to see — Liiiights Ooouuu-t Luuuu-kens!* The boy dropped the towel off his head to around his neck and entered the tube the way his teammates had, only lower into the crouch with a slower, more duck-like motion, knocking back each low five as though it was a personal invitation deserving a personal response. By the time he reached the four other starters and

James Baker Hall

commenced the bumpings, the much-debated thirty-second finale fireworks was in full bloom in the arena skies as usual, a scene right out of the Star-Spangled Banner, with combat-ready troops in evidence everywhere. Coach J.C. was introduced, probably, but not even the announcer guy who did it was sure it got done. Everything leading up to the moment of the boy's introduction that night of the season's opener in Rupp was like the first letter or two of pan-de-mon-i-um, and what happened thereafter spelled out the experience. A Richter-seven earthquake could have Xed Lex that night between 7:55 and 8:05 for all anybody would have known or cared, until the flashing, crackling, booming spectacle ceased and the smoke cleared, and the threes and fives resumed surveillance. The referee wanted to delay throwing up the ball until his whistle could be heard, but the tv people wouldn't let him —

The first few seconds of that first game of the Year of LO entered the iconography of b-ball history alongside the clip of Jimmy Valvano tearing across the floor, arms wide with joy at the end of NC State's national championship game — pictures that no one seemed to tire of seeing — the boy a kind of Nike Swoosh with the details put back in, culminating in what came to be known as the Lukens Leap, a rocket-legger that got measured and re-measured off the many pictures of it at forty-plus inches. This image became the season's logo, looped into the run-up of every televised college game in the country, and looped into the sign-off, telling the Year of LO story, and selling the season of seasons, the upshot of Lights Out Likens and Barbarsweet Zee going head-to-head off the tip, ending with the skied boy up where the fireworks had been, his lassoing left arm stirring up the wafting smoke, his big shaved head a scream of gap-toothed triumph. He'd jumped that high before and would again — never with so many watching, though — but the height was only the half of it, if that. His moment up there among the constellations went on and on, like a freeze frame, but it wasn't a freeze frame, it was the boy doing what the boy did, airing it out as only he could. When he came back down, thirty seconds into the game, he was still twirling his rope and the crowd was off the scale, the bull-moose-loony bonkers of a night full of fans gone crazy. At 6'9" 250, the athletic Barzee was the defensive hammer and shot-blocker of choice among all those in the know, and every one of them would have told you that whatever happened in this much-talked-about match-up, what did happen wasn't going to. Dunk on Barzee, forget it — you might be able to score off him, emphasis on *might,* but only a jump-shooter in the open court, one with a quick release coming off a screen. Nobody was going to score off of Barbarsweet Zee in the paint, and certainly not around the rim. The boy Lukens grabbed the ball out of the air off the tip with a little help from Ali Ali Akbar and wrap-around arms protected it without his feet moving until the flurry around him had dispersed, and all that was left of it was the crouching Barzee hungry to pounce. Face on face, they looked like the letter *M,* as in Mayday, with the one-handed ball swinging at the end of the boy Lukens' long left arm, a cat-toy pendulum back and forth, both of them obviously pleased by how quickly and cleanly the situation had reduced itself to its essentials. For several seconds they remained thus, a few strides inside Kentucky's half of the court, a few strides from the sideline, a spell-bound press row on the right side of the screen, Anjelica diJames prominently seated (Buford didn't know she was back in town until he saw her sitting there taking it all in), the house gone suddenly quiet: the two humongous athletes eyeing each other as though they too, like everyone watching, including the rest of the players on the court, were hypnotized by what was taking place. Tick tock, hickory dock went the pendulum with the little air-filled ball at the end of it. Then the boy commenced Rondo-ing college basketball's Defensive Player Year, dribbling up in his face and then backing off, getting him on one hip and then the other with a hint of the teasing that would come later, stutter-stepping him, advancing the ball toward the basket three steps and then back two, to the left between his legs and then back to the right, to the left again and then back between the legs to the right, probing, yes, measuring his opponent's quickness, yes, locating his opponent's time and place of balance, yes, clocking his feet, ahh now, yes sir, clock the dude's feet, you got feet, Sweet Zee, show me feet — but not really. Buford probably wasn't the only one who knew what he and the millions of sports fans world-wide were watching: the boy knew coming into the game he could break Barzee down off the dribble, or he discovered it when they were looking each other in the eye-ball face, before the first stutter-step, or with the first stutter-step, or the second. Withholding his face-up money move, the yoyo-dribble that would have screwed up the dude's nervous system — the boy was toying with the bugger, giving everyone a chance to calm down and give the hype a rest and get used to reality; he was setting the stage for a real contest, a test that meant something. Breaking the bugger down off the dribble could wait, the boy wanted to find out what there was to all this Barzee muscle talk — so there they went to the hoop, the big, mean hammer, the boy, and the ball: like they were all one glorious, uprising DNAish thing: swirling and thrashing body parts looking for a shape, until the boy's left hand emerged at the top with the ball in its palm, voila, like a cherry on top of a sundae — frozen there momentarily, or so it surely seemed, an impression confirmed on replay, a moment out of time you were called to notice — before he threw el sweet cherry ball into the hole with a mighty thonk and rattle, leaving the very hammer on his athletic powder-blue backside sliding into the photographers. The cry of triumph so-called — actually it was

James Baker Hall

a howl of joy — came on the boy as he was circling back up the floor, and the lassoing Lukens Leap launched him *a la* Cape Kennedy at the free-throw line, occasioning the first of the glory-year tape measures and stop watches. That was how the UK season of seasons commenced, with everyone in the sports world worldwide watching unranked UK's finesse player hammer second-ranked UNC's hammer onto to his powder-blue ass, on the way to an 18-point victory.

Joe Survant

The Angel

Here is the time that can be uttered, here is its home. Speak
and confirm. More than ever things are falling away...

Rilke, *The Ninth Elegy*

The angel floats
like a maple seed
above the ground.
She drifts over
dense thickets bright
with the flowers
of blackberries
and over
orderly regiments
of grass, gathering
lawn by lawn.

She even sees
the common yarrow
as it spreads along the road,
how slender its wand,
how finely divided its leaves.
Yet she will not touch them.
Neither will she walk
on the freckled ground,
even as lightly as the
parachutes of dandelions
drifting behind enemy lines.

We must not believe
in her who passes
through our bodies
and through the earth
disturbing no particle of atom.
She will not teach us

Joe Survant

the knotted language of thistle,
which we must know.
She will not take us
under the hill,
where we must go.

After My Father's Illness

I sit in the prow
to watch
for rocks and snags.
The canoe seems
lighter than the leaves
curled up like hulls
on the unclear stream.
We pass them
with no noise.

Here in red September
the river seems
a lid of ice,
our blue canoe
some skater stretching
out to glide.

My father guides
with long strokes.
His breath is even.
Beneath the surface
I hear the deep machinery
of water on rock
and see a field
unfold with rolls
of millet and rye.
The varnish smell

of mold rises
in shafts of light
to meet the sky.

I must not turn
and look behind.
It's just death
he says.

Owl

The owl glides in
on secret wings,
silent as leaf flush.
He knows the quick
motives of chipmunks,
the intimacy of mice.
A cloud of clacking crows follows
full of anger and fear.
They blow around him
like ashes from a fire.
Why do they hate his loneliness?

I have come too far today.
The paths of deer
have deceived me
with thicket and briar.
I strain to hear
the whine and tear
of their intricate voices.
Stormy crows
rise up
to wheel and jeer
at my quietly brooding owl.

Maya

The cattle stand facing east.
Their bodies shine like lumps
of coal in the rising sun.
They stand in the center of the worn

geometry of their paths. Sun
warms their black hides, making
light upon them tremble.
Hard hooves have vanished.

Around them the yellow heads
of dandelions collapse and rid
themselves of ragged bodies
rising from milky roots.

Nearby the tight brown coats
of cattails emphatic on the margins
of the pond have begun to dissolve
into flakes of air-borne down.

I am here watching, wearing
my heaviness like a coat.
Hard matter in its home around
me seems poised to disappear.

Benediction

We are grateful
the deer have returned.
Their stillness
fills the woods.
The dog stretches.
The cat arches her back
in appreciation.

We are grateful
the deer have returned.
Squash glows
like a secret
in the garden.
Rain gathers
upon the beans.

We are grateful
the deer have returned.
They stir memories
so old
we make noises
almost human.

Joe Survant

Disturbing a Nest

In a patch of woods
between my house and street
the ground squirms.
Two-inch quail
dart away
on quick feet,
the hen hidden, still
as a leaf.

In my hurry
I had forgotten
the woodpecker's code,
did not hear
the thrush
in the shadbush tree
beating like
a speckled heart.

I stop all that I do
to let them pass,
nine small quail moving
through the morning grass.

Letter to RPW On His 100th Birthday

In this century, and moment, of mania,
Tell me a story.
                    Audubon: A Vision

It is another century, another moment now
but blood still cries for blood,
its stamen, its terrible cloying flower.

Those given Absolute Knowledge
still hone it like a knife
worked carefully across a stone

while those who would never
profess such certainty
are stricken, even to the bone.

Yet the story does not change.
A boy in the dark still hears
the great geese hoot northward

and rushes into the heart's fine ignorance
on a dirt road, in Kentucky, where
ironweed prospers, and its stem grows hard.

The parched corn still lifts
its sharp arms in the heat,
keeps secret its cloistered core

while the boy strips the crisp, green husk
seeking the sweet juices,
the kerneled mystery, always more and more.

He smells the wild narcotic leaves
hanging dryly in the barns
and the grass when it rises, and when it dies.

Despite the knives and broiling blood
winter wheat still glows like glass
and hay falls quietly in the fields, fodder where it lies.

Joe Survant

When the Great House is Broken

When the great house
is broken,
lupine and bursting heart
are lost
while streets assert
their rigid geometry,
and whole cities
sit at attention.

When the great house
is broken,
people take up their boulders
while memory root
sprouts indifferent as fur
upon their shoulders,
and their deep woods
clamor with longing.

When the great house
is broken,
wedges of high-blown geese
come apart
and yellow winds
flush out
the hidden coveys
of small quail.

When the great house
is broken,
horses in the field
lean toward the whisper
of frozen grass,
the tangled hearts
of weeds explode
and are laid bare.

Upon the Water's Face

Alma Lee Medley
1908-1997

My mother's last sister
sits in a worn, green rowboat
folding and refolding her hands.
They signal as
the boat moves out.
Our few words scatter
like little herds of waves.

She is drifting away,
her husband
thirty years ahead.
Remember the picnics
on your big screened porch?
Even Uncle Tommy..., I begin.
Who are you? she asks.

She is moving further out,
the wind is eating all our words.
Then I see it, a long brown
rope trailing the boat.
I reach out to draw her back,
but it is only a strand of moss
dissolving in my hands.

Anne Waters

May 1, 1882

The way wood grows
smooth with use,
the way hands
harden against wood,
the way we've worn
around each other.
Alph and I grown
alternately smooth and hard,
each shaping and
being shaped
in the play
of will on will.
But now we've
grown peaceful
with old age.
The fire rises, then
falls into itself
making a little
cave of dark.
In the quiet thicket
below the house
honeysuckle in yearly
measure constricts
and winds
by small degrees
the living trunk
of a sassafras tree.

Alpheus Waters

June 5, 1882

Mountain Boy parts this
muddy river like a plow,
water washed thick with
topsoil from the fields.
I love the power of its
wheel, and blades that
drive us up the stream
to Hawesville.
Owensboro's yellow banks
have long since fallen behind
and the Ohio lies before us
like an undiscovered land.

Sand Island hides the
Indiana shore and seems
to move with us in the mist.
Blue herons stalk the shallows
taking fish and frogs with
sudden snakelike strikes.
Crows call to each other
in their harsh language
and ducks move by
in tight formations.

Over everything the current flows.
Never losing its patience
it growls past the boat's prow
and makes a wake
at all the snags.

Riding through the river
of air, the sun and moon
cast their own currents
on the water, on the shore,
and on us all.

The Golden Circumstance

Sallie

I saw Autumn coming toward me
in a golden dress green-hemmed,
with scarlet petticoat. I looked
right through her and saw the old forest

inside her trees. I looked and
I was she. I heard then the
ancient languages of elms about
to be forgotten and the words of men

already fallen from memory.
Around me the urgent voices
of sapling redbud and sassafras
were like a choir of locusts. I felt

the dying maple blaze in the distance
and smelled the dark wet ashes
of the earth. I tasted winter in
my mouth like a strong lover.

Then I began to turn and dance
within my golden circumstance.

Tongues of Light

Sallie

This morning the voices were clanging
bells within me, and each one
brought a face, some frowning, some grinning,
until I could neither hear nor see

what was around me, the soughing wind
in the trees, the graceful turn of the leaves.
I was sucked into myself. The world
and all its pieces disappeared.

The voices all spoke together
and the faces crowded inside me.
They called in the names of confusion,
in words like swarming bees

until one said softer than the rest,
Open your ears to hear, your eyes to see.
Then I heard the forest burning with
its million leaves turning like the pages

of a book. And as I looked
I heard the subtle tongues of light,
the meanings of the leaves as they said,
Yellow, orange, red.

Robin Floyd Remembers His First Trip

I was pulling the stern oar.
Dad was piloting. We'd been out a while
when we struck a hidden rock.
My oar swung round

and threw me in the river. I
struggled to rise, but the raft was running
above me. When I popped up
behind the raft, Dad threw me
a rope and we kept on running. But I
wasn't strong enough to handle an oar,
and we took a terrible pounding
at Drum's Back Rock, then
the current swept us against Blue
Bluff. Daddy said, *Pull*
the oar, boy! and I tried
but couldn't. The raft hit the bluff
and the current held us and beat us
against it. The raft was coming apart
so I jumped and swam hard
to the roots of a big sycamore
standing on the other side. I
climbed out in the cold and saw
Daddy still on the heaving raft.
I yelled, *Get off there,*
Dad, it's breaking!
But the logs he stood on parted
and he went down between them.
I yelled again and he
came up swimming. The river
swept him along and I followed
running. I met him at the bank
and the raft went on down
the river. We watched it go
then hurried to warm ourselves
in my uncle's house a mile
up Wolf Pen Creek.
It was my first trip.
Already I was in love with the river.

Sena Jeter Naslund

The Perfecting of the Chopin *Valse No. 14 in E Minor*

One day last summer when I was taking a shower, I heard my mother playing the Chopin *Valse No. 14 in E Minor* better than she ever had played it before. Twenty years ago in Birmingham, I had listened to her while I sat on dusty terra cotta tiles on the front porch. I was five, and I remember looking up from my dirty foot to see the needle of a hummingbird entering one midget blossom after another, the blossoms hanging like froth on our butterfly bush. Probably my mother had first practiced the *Valse* thirty years or so before that, in Missouri, when she was a child, in a living room close enough to a dirt road to hear wagons passing, close enough for dust to sift over the piano keys. How was it that after knowing the piece for over fifty years, my mother suddenly was playing it better than she ever had in her life?

I turned off the shower to make sure. It was true. There was a bounce and yet a delicacy in the repeated notes at the beginning of the phrase that she had never achieved before. And then the flight of the right hand up the keyboard was like the gesture of a dancer lifting her arm, unified and lilting. I waited for the double *forte*, which she never played loudly enough, and heard it roar out of the piano and up the furnace pipe to the bathroom. Perhaps that was it: the furnace pipe was acting like a

Sena Jeter Naslund

natural amplifier, like a speaking tube. Dripping wet, I stepped over the tub and walked through the bathroom door to the landing at the top of the stairs. She was at the section with the *alberti*-like bass. Usually her left hand hung back, couldn't keep the established tempo here (and it had been getting worse in the last seven or so years), but the left hand cut loose with the most perfectly rolled over *arpeggio* I had ever heard. Rubinstein didn't do it any better.

I hurried down the steps; she was playing the repeated notes again as one of the recapitulations of the opening phrase came up. I tried to see if she had finally decided to use Joseffy's suggested fingering—2, 4, 5, 1,—instead of her own 4, 3, 2, 1 on which she had always insisted. But I was just too late to see. She finished with a flourish.

"Bravo!" I shouted and clapped. The water flew out of my hands like a wet dog shaking his fur. She leaned over the piano protectively.

"You're getting the keys wet," she said, smiling.

"You played that so well!"

"Suppose the milkman comes while you're naked?"

"Didn't you think you played it well?"

"I'm improving. You always do, from time to time."

"This was super."

"Thank you," she said, and got up to make her second cup of coffee.

"Did you remember to take Hydropres?" I yelled. She is quite deaf, but refused to wear her hearing aid while she practices. *You know how music sounds over the telephone*, she said to me once; that was what a hearing aid did to sounds.

"Did you take H?" I shouted a little louder.

She threw one of her white sweaters over the Walter Jackson Bate biography of Keats. "Don't read the last two chapters late at night," she said. "It makes you too sad."

I had taken to reading about Romantic poets and their poetry, too, to relieve the glassy precision of my work at the pharmaceutical lab. I left the books around, and as she had done since I was a child, she read what I read—usually two hundred pages ahead of me. I put on her sweater, its wool sticking to my damp skin.

And I forgot about the *Valse in E Minor*. Maybe that performance was a fluke. Maybe I was mistaken.

It was not long after this that a rock in the garden began to move. It was thigh high and pockmarked, and the pocks were rimmed with mica. The arcs of mica had the same curve as a fingernail clipping or the curve of a glittering eyelash.

Our garden was on a small scale by Louisville standards— about fifty-by-forty feet. We had landscaped it, though—rather expensively for us. A stucco wall hung between four brick columns across the back. Herringbone-brick walks were flanked by clumps of iris, day lilies and chrysanthemums so that we had

Sena Jeter Naslund

spots of spring, summer and fall bloom. There was a small statue of a girl looking up at the sky and spreading her stone apron to catch the rain. The apron was a birdbath. It was that sort of yard. Pretty, costly per square foot, designed to console us for our lack of scope. I had some dwarf fruit trees across the back, in front of the stucco wall.

The previous owner had had the mica boulder placed over a large chipmunk hole so no one would accidentally step in. The placement was imperfect aesthetically, and my mother said it ought to be moved, but I didn't want to go to the bother to hire somebody to do it. Sometimes I'd see her lean against the rock, her basket full of the spent heads of iris or day lilies, or windfall apples, or other garden debris. We were neat.

One bright night when the mica was arcing in the moonlight, I saw her going out there in her pajamas. She carried one of the rose satin sofa cushions, and its sides gleamed in the light. She put the cushion on top of the rock, climbed up, and sat on it. She looked like a bird sitting on a giant egg, a maharini riding an elephant, a child on a Galapagos tortoise.

I felt unreal, frightened, standing beside the bedroom curtain peering out. And stunned. I sat down on the bed, touched another satin cushion, smoothed it, soothed it. I held the cool satin against my cheeks. My tears made dark blotches on the fabric. I wanted to lie down, to deny her madness in the garden. And I did. I turned the cushion to the dry side, lay down on it and went to sleep.

In the morning the teakettle shrieked, she poured the water for her instant coffee, called "Good morning" to me, and all was ordinary.

While I walked in the garden, I noticed the rock had shifted. Around the base was a crescent of damp stone where crumbs of still-moist earth clung. The boulder had rotated a little, as though Antarctica on a giant globe had slipped northward a hundred miles into the South Pacific. Perhaps the rock had been more precariously balanced than I had thought. Perhaps her weight had caused it to shift—a slow-motion version of a child sitting on a big beach ball.

But from that morning on I began to see a change in her health. She was tired. She was less ready to smile, and her eyes took on a hurt quality. Each day she seemed to get up later. She asked to eat out, and she ate ravenously, at Italian restaurants. She ate like a runner—huge quantities of pasta.

But the food did no good. Each day she was weaker.

And each day the ugly earthy area on the rock rose higher and higher out of the ground. What had been a slight crescent of dirt became a huge black island covering several thousand miles in the Hawaii area.

She changed her diet from high carbohydrate to high protein. I wanted to speak to her about her eating, but it was as

Sena Jeter Naslund

though there was a bandage across my mouth.

I tried once, in the kitchen, to say, "Mama, why are you eating in this crazy way?" But all I could say was, "Mmmm, Mmmm."

She glanced at me in that quick, hurt way, and I hushed.

Then the gag seemed to change its location. Instead of being across my mouth, it seemed to be tied on top of my head and to pass under my chin. It was the kind of bandage you see on the dead in nineteenth-century etchings—something to hold the jaw closed, something Jacob Marley might have been wearing when he first appeared to Scrooge. Again, I felt it in the kitchen. I tried to say, "Mama, Mama, what are you doing to yourself? Why are you so tired?" But I couldn't even drop my jaw, couldn't get my mouth open for a murmur.

That night I stayed awake to watch the rock. At midnight, I knelt on my bed and peered out the window. There was no human form perched on the rock. Nevertheless I watched and watched. About 1:00, when I was quite drowsy, the rock suddenly glittered. It was as though the mica were catching light at a new angle. Sometimes this happens if a lamp is turned on in the house, or one is turned off. But there was no change in the lighting and yet this sudden sparkling, flashing out of light. My mouth tried to open in a silent and spontaneous *Oh!*, but it was as though the binding cloth were in place. I was not permitted this small gesture of surprise.

Then I saw her rise up from behind the rock. She moved very slowly. Her movement was the kind I make in dreams when I feel panic, panic and also a heaviness, an inertia that scarcely permits forward motion. Her shoulders stooping, her hands and arms hanging like weights, she slowly began to walk down the bricks toward the house. I wanted to leap to meet her, to tell her, to tell her, *Nevermind. Nevermind, you don't have to do it, I'll hire a crane, I'll hire the neighborhood boys, I'll hire a doctor day and night, don't try this, here, here let me help.* But I was immobilized.

The cloths that had bound shut my jaw now bound my entire body. I could not flex my knees. I tried to heave myself off the bed; I would roll to her help. But my body was as rigid as a statue.

I was forced to remain kneeling on the coverlet, looking out the window, watching her toiling past the ruddy day lilies. At a certain point, she passed beyond my sight line. There were three small steps there; and my ears strained to tell me that she had negotiated them all right, that now she was opening the storm door, now she was coming in from the night, that she had not fallen at the last moment, that she was not lying hurt right at her own safe door, that she had not struck her head on the steps—but my hearing failed, too. All of my senses were suddenly gone, as though I had received a blow to the head.

I awoke in the early hours to a loud thunderclap. The weather was changing early. It was late summer, and the fall rains

Sena Jeter Naslund

were coming. Our air seemed like the ice water you stand strips of carrots and celery in to crisp. Day lilies were drooping and the chrysanthemums straining upright, ready to grow and take over the garden. I checked the statue of the girl. Serrated yellow leaves from a neighboring elm had blown into her apron.

The boulder had rotated 180 degrees from its original position. The black cap rode at the north pole. Below it the rock was clean and traces of mica sparkled in the sunlight. But I fancied the darkness was spreading, an earthen glaciation coming down to nullify the brightness of human accomplishment.

I knew it was hopeless to attempt to ask her any questions. Even as I tried mentally to formulate an inquiry, my body stiffened. I resisted that stillness. I would not be frozen into stone in my own garden in late summer. I would not take on that terrible rigidity. I would not allow my body to imagine death.

Her health began to improve, but it gave me no joy. I knew that this improvement was temporary. That August, gesturing toward the garden, a friend who raised berries told me that death was part of life; she pointed at the seasonal changes. We stood on the patio talking while the Chopin *Valse No. 14* rolled out the windows.

I explained that each time my mother played it now, it was better. Sometimes it was improved only by the way a single note was played, but suddenly that note, once dead, leaped into life. And then the next time, the notes around it would be more vital, would be like flowers straining toward the light, inspired by one of their number who had risen above them. The whole surface of the music was becoming luminous.

I told my friend that the gulf between the seasonal lives of flowers and the lives of human beings was unbridgeable. The *forte* drowned out my voice, a *forte* big enough now to fill the garden.

Our garden was the perfect place for a garden party, but I had never had one there. I preferred to have one friend over at a time, or two. But two weeks after the weather change, I discovered that invitations had been issued to almost every person of my acquaintance to join me *and the chrysanthemums* for a gourmet dinner. *Gourmet!* To join me and the chrysanthemums! They weren't ready!

As usual, I had worked late at the laboratory. When I came out to the car, the pink glow of the sunset was reflected in the windshield. Amidst the wash of pink, a folded card had been placed under the wiper: an invitation for six o'clock. It was already half-past six. There wasn't a potato chip in the house, and we'd eaten our last TV entrée; I was supposed to get more on the way home. While I stood there fingering the stiff paper, I realized how many people had smiled at me that day, had said *See you later* or *Looking forward to it* or *Thanks for asking*—all mysterious, muttered fragments scattered over the day, everybody being especially gracious to me, or worse, *encouraging*.

Sena Jeter Naslund

Could I run home, maybe cook flowers? I was a very poor cook; my mother was no cook. We had long benefited from eating out and from TV dinners. They were the expensive TV dinners—pretty and tasty, even if always too salty.

As I sped home, I thought that at least my mother would be there to greet them. Like an illuminated billboard, the invitation flashed at me again. I recognized the handwriting. It was her writing. Large letters, angular, the capital A half-printed, looking like a star.

There were so many cars that I had to drive past the house looking for parking. Other latecomers—there was my supervisor—were sauntering down the sidewalks toward home. I parked almost two blocks away.

As I walked home as fast as I could, half a block away, I smelled the party. I gasped. Yes, my jaw *was* allowed to drop in amazement: *Oh!* heavenly aromas.

There was roast beef! No, not just roast beef— something richer, more savory. Beef Wellington. I could envision the pastry head of a steer decorating its flank. But the odor of bacon, too, why bacon? It couldn't be, but there was a choice of entrees, just like when we had two separate frozen Stouffers. Trout was broiling under strips of bacon. There! There was a waft of garlic butter, for escargot.

And desserts had been freshly baked. That was angel food cake in the air, and there was the sweet cinnamon of apple brown Betty, and there, the orange liqueur that goes *flambé* with *crepes suzette*. She had prepared three desserts. But you can't just have main courses and desserts! Where were the vegetables? She had forgotten the vegetables. Memory *was* becoming uncertain: I *had* heard her hesitate to enter the second theme of the *Valse*.

My supervisor was poised at the head of our walk, sniffing. I shouldered past him.

"Vegetables?" I exclaimed.

"Who cares?" He inhaled deeply.

I managed to make myself enter the house quietly. There was that civilized murmur in the room. The sound you hear in the finest restaurants, the bliss of conversation elevated by the artistry of food, of the tongue bending this way and that in ecstasy.

There she stood chatting, her hearing aid in place. She who had been reclusive, a devotee of music alone, for years. I noticed there was a dusting of flour on her hands and arms, up to her elbows. She seemed unaware of the flour, stood relaxed and comfortable as though she were wearing a pair of evening gloves.

"Mother," I said, "are you all right?"

She reached out and squeezed my elbow. Her grip was steadying. "Of course," she said. "I was just telling your friend

Sena Jeter Naslund

we should have parties more often. I'm enjoying myself so much."

"All this food?" I said lamely.

"I can read a book, as you know. I got down James Beard, Irma Rombauer. I hadn't looked in Fanny for years."

"Are there any vegetables?"

"Sautéed celery, new peas in sherry sauce." She pointed at some covered dishes. "Here comes the mailman."

Other people began to arrive. People I had lost track of years before. How did she find them? I started to ask, but the hinge of my jaw began to resist; the familiar paralysis gently threatened. Questions had become out of order.

My salivary glands prompted me. Eat, *eat*. She had my plate ready for me—flamboyant and multi-colored. It held something of everything. When I inhaled, I seemed to levitate six or seven inches—or float, that feeling you get walking neck deep in a swimming pool on your big toes. Glancing down, I saw my food had been arranged on a new plate, the tobacco-leaf pattern that I had admired in the Metropolitan Museum catalogue. Seventy-nine dollars *per*. And each guest had one. I was rich.

One guest held no tobacco-leaf plate. Indeed, he wasn't eating. I didn't know him, had never known him, I was quite sure. He was standing beside the piano talking with mother. He was grossly fat, with reddish hair, what was left of it; he was mostly bald. Only his nose seemed familiar. It was a large and romantic proboscis, lean and humped—no, arched. They were discussing fingering. Mother was drumming the air—4, 3, 2, 1—and he was responding 4, 3, 2, 1. But then on one, he gave the rug a quick jab with this foot. Ah, he was suggesting the last of the repeated notes be quickly pedalled. What an idea! Joseffy certainly never hints at such an effect.

Mother looked delighted. She too jabbed the rug with her foot. No, he shook his head, *not quite fast enough*. He actually reached over and grasped her right leg above the knee, grasped the quadricep muscle and forced a quick tap of the imaginary *sostenuto* pedal. Now he was savoring the unheard sound. With his face tilted up in the lamplight, I suddenly recognized him. At least I recognized a part of him. It was the nose of Frederick Chopin.

My mouth fell open. It was to gasp, I thought. But instead these words fell out, double *forte*, "Let's all go into the garden now." And I rotated—gracefully, I could tell—to lead the way through the French doors. But why, when the chrysanthemums weren't ready?

The garden was ablaze in torchlight. Real torches, like the Statue of Liberty holds up, but with long handles planted in the ground or jutting out from the back wall, torches like you see in some paintings of the garden of Gethsemane with that rich

Sena Jeter Naslund

Dutch light flickering everywhere. And the chrysanthemums had been multiplied.

No longer just my neat mounds of red cushion mums. There was rank on rank of mums of all colors and forms, spider mums in oranges and yellows. Giant football mums in purples, lavenders and whites, star-burst mums, fireballs and a thousand tiny button mums massed against the stucco wall. All the guests were gasping with delight. They hurried to stand among them, cupped individual blossoms like the chins of favored children; long index fingers pointed through the flickering light at flowers just beyond. When the guests knelt to study whole clumps, their bodies disappeared among the rows of flowers and their heads floated among them, heads themselves like large flowers or cabbages. Above us smiled the crescent moon.

I wanted to turn, to say *Mother, come look, come join us, they are so beautiful, thank you, thank you, they have never been so beautiful,* and of course I could not turn back. My body gasped with grief. The dreadful *rigor* seized me. Then all that was replaced with the turbulence and then the gaiety of the Chopin *Valse No. 14 in E Minor.*

Could I hold my breath throughout? Could I thus make the moment permanent? Could I make the air hold that music forever, vivid as a painting, more permanent than stone, sound becoming statuary of the air? And would the performance be perfect at last? Who played? Was it *he* or *she?*

I held my breath on and on as each passage of loveliness, the lightest, most gay of sounds, swept past. But where was the pedal touch on the fourth of the repeated notes? Of course it was withheld, withheld till the phrase was introduced for the last time, and then the pedal, a suggestion of poignant prolonging, a *soupçon* of romantic rubato, a wobble in rhythm, the human touch in the final offering of art. Then it ended.

Then, only then, the air rushed from my lungs. "BRAVO!," I shouted. Unbound, my jaw seemed to be permitted to open all the way to my heart. "HOORAY! HOORAY!" I shouted, raising my fist and punching the air over my head. All the guests shouted "BRAVO!," their fists aloft. And dozens of Roman candles, skyrockets, pinwheels shot up into the air, bust gloriously high above our heads, bloomed like flowers forced by a movie camera. I felt her standing behind me, her hand a warm squeeze on my elbow.

The next morning I found her note saying that she wanted to vacation in England. She had taken a morning flight. England because they spoke her language there. I walked into the bright garden. Of course, she had hired a clean-up crew to take away the spent torches and the mess. The gauzy crescent moon, the ghost of a thorn, hung in the blue.

I visited the rock. It had been rolled six feet west, to the artistically correct place. The dark continent had returned to the

Sena Jeter Naslund

bottom of the world, no longer visible at the juncture of rock and grass. The rock was right side up and mica glittered over its dome. Where it had stood gaped the chipmunk hole, wide enough for a human thigh. A dark, pleasant hole.

Ah, there was the chipmunk already, poising at the rim of damp earth, blinking in the sunlight.

Jane Gentry

May Weather

Because I knew you
the air shines blue as the backs
of the selfish jays bivouacking tree
to tree high up among fresh leaves
that lean out on tender necks toward
a world where colors bright as kites
against this sky pluck back their edges
sharp as the black arrows
of the jays' territorial cries

Tantalus

In my favorite picture of you, you stand
in a leafy garden in Rome, Georgia,
your sixty-five year old torso twisted
like the Apollo Belvedere, but you
rest one hand on a dry-laid wall and
the other on your hip. You wear a starched
shirt and a yellow tie. You're here
on business. You look straight
at me behind the camera, your face
alive with a smile not yet broken
open. Sun lights your face and your hand
on the stone, while a single pen
warms in your breast pocket.
Above your head, a loaded
branch dangles a firmament
of cherries, mostly ripe, promising
this summer and others sure to come.
Neither of us thinks (I, framing you
in rocks, red fruit, and foliage; you,
looking backward through the camera, focusing
on me a happiness I cannot now imagine)
that even as we dallied in that garden,

a seed, stoic as a cherry stone, was rooting
in you: would snake its branches
to your brain, its taproot to your gut.

The Blessing

Your seizures began under your bedside lamp
as you lay reading as if it were an ordinary night.
But the nightstand, the bottles of pills: Ritalin,
Tegratol, Proscar, Cepra, Colace, Temazepam.
"Something is happening," you said, and a corner
of your mouth drooped; your left eye quivered and
closed. Spasms marched across your fingers one by
one, then up your arm, into your face. I helped you
step into your khakis, buttoned up your shirt.
Under a spell, one foot in front of the other, we left

the bedroom – you, for the last time. As if
it were any Saturday night, we drove to Lexington,
drew up to the emergency room. When its glass
door slid open before us, we entered disaster's
gathering place: a man held a paper towel to his
bleeding forehead, his wife begged into a cell
phone for her mother to keep the kids just
till she could come first thing in the morning.
A whole family, tight-lipped, pale, sat and stood
around a man, his coat pulled up to hide his face.

A skinny girl, alone, rocking, shushing a limp baby,
stared anxiously at the fluorescent window
where help might call her name. Half a dozen
school boys rehearsed in awed voices
the process of their wreck that slung their buddy out
onto the pavement. A puckish, red-cheeked toddler
pulled away from her exhausted mother. At last
the window opened just a crack to let your name

come out. Finally behind the glass, we, in a tongue
learned at check-ups and check-ins, recited

the litany: melanoma, metastases, gamma knife,
bio-chemotherapy, interferon, whole-brain radiation,
—dreamily, as if this weren't your own self's
body: your calloused, useful hands; your quick eyes
that saw pictures in the world; the ladder of your back
that could raise and fling a sack of horse-feed heavier
than a man. A nurse led you to a hallway cot (all cubicles
full of hurt already). I pulled close a chair, tried to keep
the passage clear, gripped your softening hand,
tried to think what else you might have to do without.

Invisible behind a curtain, a baby set up
his primal cry, radical as a fresh-pulled root.
The doctor told the young parents to bathe him
in cool water, that his fever would go
down by morning. He would not die. And still
the baby wailed. Your own face dropped its pain,
its fear, and smiled a smile clear as good
water. "His life is just beginning. Mine is
almost done," you said. "I only hope that his will be
as rich as mine has been for me."

Winter Moon

When I open my curtains at daybreak
the fey old moon sits on a branch
ready to flap away into the half-light
above the luminous triangles
of houses in the next street.
Rising, shrinking, the bright bone
is buried then revealed again
in the slow smudge of clouds.

Intensive Care, Oncology

Swept up in our own storm, still we registered
the fact of Hurricane Katrina aimed like a
gun to rip New Orleans. The television,
incessantly updating, floated like a window
by Magritte in the air above your bed. Next
morning, your treatment starting, we could be
happy that the levies held the surge. You then
lay flat, as ordered, tubes plugged into your port,

felt briefly, finally like yourself as nurses
loosed the poisonous current in your blood.
By your bed, anchored to your hand (still useful,
calloused), I watched the riptide wash you
under. One moment you were
there; the next, in watery fluorescent light
your body lay as empty of yourself as your
shoes and jacket in the wardrobe by the sink.

The Lamp

The new moon, the ghost of a ghost, floats
below the surface in a cold sea
of cloud. When you died after months
of longing, the moon was full, and I still
felt the holiness of your presence
in the room where the long chain
of your breath broke. For days after,
you made the lamp, untouched, light,
and then go dark. I was spent, afraid, full
of you, your absence. And I unplugged
the lamp. Now, of course, I long
for any sliver of poor light.

The Berry Bowls

Spring was your last season. Now it's here
again with its clatter of birds, with its promises
moving on the air, while the world closes
like water over the roofs of the deserted village
of your life. Last May I watched you shed
our necessary illusions of safety and sure
time, just as, after hard frost,
a tree lets go its leaves.

Earlier, in our fog of loss, we stopped
at a yard sale. For my sake
you feigned interest in six berry bowls
I bought, their gilded fruit ghost-like
from long use. By then you'd seen
your name on all the shards of ostracism—
you faced already toward the border
of another country. You knew you would not
sit in this spring's sun eating breakfast
from these bowls, their dimming gold.

Crossing from Providence to Newport

Cresting the Claiborne Pell Bridge, I drive
straight into the pearly pink
sunrise, where one planet pulses
clear as a holy promise. Sailboats
moored to left and right ride
the iridescence of Narragansett Bay
on which a cruise ship floats
in tiers like a wedding cake.

What promises I used to see
in such a sight. But then your body
drew into a claw, nurses drew

Jane Gentry

your blood, punctured your scalp
with the crown and gamma knife.

Now I come to see your daughter
married. When you heard "cancer"
your great grief was for your absence
here. But this bride's day
will rise to noon, and the world
gives what it gives: my eyes
are mine, but see
through yours as well.

From My Passing Car I See
In the Cemetery

black winter trees against the snow,
rows of stones, each topping a mound
pillowy as a new-made bed.
Under two of these, side by side lies
what remains of my mother and my father,
not spooned as they slept
when I fled to their bed from a childish
dream, but stiff, formal as relief
upon sarcophagi, so cold that they've lost
touch as surely as Odysseus and his mother
did when in the Underworld he reached out
to hold her and she dissolved like smoke.
Just so, my parents lost their flesh, the hair
on their arms (hers bright, his dark);
their cheeks (hers like silk, his like sand),
collapsed; the bowls of their skulls
empty now; the fountains of their breaths
stopped; their sturdy bones deconstructing
molecule by molecule, down in the dark
under this blanket of snow, clasped
in the black arms of the black trees.

Crows

As metaphor for thought and mind
I thought of crows in winter trees,
riding ragged branches through the wind,
as raucous before roost as words.

By threes, by twos, then one by one
they leave my vacant mind to comb
with hungry teeth the tangled skies
and circle home, past sight, beyond the rise.

Empty tree, whipped by the wind,
old head, stand metaphor for mind.

Sleeping in the Bed with Jake, My Three-Year-Old Grandson

You curl backward in the curve of my body,
your head under my nose, your fresh body
hot as a sausage, your scent flaming from
your scalp, the roots of your hair, and I revel
as in a flower, its petals licking my nostrils.

My sleep beside your sleep lightens when you
pitch yourself around in bed like a sparking
pinwheel's pleasure in itself, or a puzzle
piece shifting for its own fit.

I wake near dawn because the round
stone of your head butts against my back,
its deep heat burning through my gown.
That fire sunk in the rock of yourself
will not gutter until I've long gone
dark and cold. Even then those tongues,
orange and indigo, may sometimes say
my name.

Jane Gentry

In the First Hour of Your Life

I am a cliché. Grandmother: gray, good,
half-blind, bloodless as a greeting card.
But 600 miles away I felt your surge as you burst
from the darkness of my daughter's body, drawing
after you the blood-filled sac you grew in, from
which you butted through the gate
of bone into the light.

In your first hour I think about your
last, and pray those gates of horn swing
gently for you, finished with your life, not
easy because it will have been a human life,
but filled with sun upon your face,
snow in wakes around your quiet steps, and
spills of rain through fields you walked in.

In this first hour of your life I think
of much-loved bodies fallen back to darkness,
whose blood is quick and fresh in your new
veins, in you whose flesh re-gathers theirs.

In your first hour I am far away,
but, more than thought or kindly sentiment,
I am a body, once new as yours.
My old flesh hungers now to hurry to
you, to behold black depths
in your voracious eyes astonished
at such light, in your first hour.

About the Writers:

Richard Taylor teaches English at Kentucky State University in Frankfort. He is the author of five collections of poetry, two novels, and several non-fiction books. Formerly a poet laureate of Kentucky (1999-2001), he and his wife own and operate Poor Richard's Books in Frankfort. Growing up in Louisville, he earned a Ph.D. in English from the University of Kentucky and a J.D. degree from Brandeis School of Law at the University of Louisville. He formerly worked in the Poetry-in-the-Schools Program for the Kentucky Arts Council, and was a teacher and dean of the Governor's Scholars Program. He has just finished a book on Abraham Lincoln's connection to Kentucky which will be published this spring as a special issue of *Back Home in Kentucky*. Last year the University Press of Kentucky published his novel *Sue Mundy, A Novel of the Civil War*, a fictionalized treatment of the life and times of Marcellus Jerome Clarke, the most notorious Confederate guerrilla in Kentucky during the Civil War. He is currently working on a collection of "rough sonnets" on Abraham Lincoln called *Rail Splitter*.

James Baker Hall lives on the edge of the Bluegrass, in Sadieville, twenty-five miles north of his hometown of Lexington, Kentucky. He taught English and creative writing at the University of Kentucky for thirty years. He is the author of several volumes of poetry – *Stopping on the Edge to Wave* (Wesleyan University Press*), Fast Signing Mute* (Larkspur Press), *The Mother on the Other Side of the World* (Sarabande Books), and *The Total Light Process: New & Selected Poems* (University Press of Kentucky). He is also the author of a novel-in-verse, *Praeder's Letters* (Sarabande Books). His poems have been published individually in *The New Yorker, The Paris Review, Poetry, The American Poetry Review, The Kenyon Review*, and elsewhere. Mr. Hall has received an NEA fellowship in poetry, and won both the Pushcart and O. Henry prizes. He took his B.A. at the University of Kentucky, in 1957, and his M.A. at Stanford University, in 1961. He is also a much respected photographer.

Joe Survant grew up in Owensboro, Kentucky, on the Ohio River. On an NDEA Fellowship he attended the University of Delaware where he received his Ph.D. in 1970. In 2007 he retired from Western Kentucky University after thirty-eight years of teaching, the majority of that time at Western, where he helped establish its creative writing program. On a Fulbright Fellowship in 1983-84, he taught at the Universiti Sains Malaysia (in Penang, Malaysia.) His collection of poems, *The Presence of Snow in the Tropics*, came out of that year in SE Asia.

After years as an academic, largely neglecting his poetry, he began to write and publish poems in earnest in the late 1980s, jumpstarted by his year in Malaysia. In 1995, he won the State Street Press Poetry Prize where his first collection, *We Will All Be Changed*, was published. His second book, a collection of narrative poems, *Anne & Alpheus, 1842-1882*, a story of rural life in south central Kentucky, won the 1996 Arkansas Poetry Prize from the University of Arkansas Press. In 2001, Landmark Books of Singapore published *The Presence of Snow in the Tropics*. In 2002, the University Press of Florida published a second collection of narrative poems, *Rafting Rise*, a story of log rafting and a river witch in the Green River Basin of the early 20th century. He served as Kentucky's Poet Laureate from 2002 to 2004.

Sena Jeter Naslund began writing when she was a child. Her impulse to write was a reflection of her love of reading such books as the Laura Ingalls Wilder *Little House on the Prairie* series, Louisa May Alcott's *Little Women*, and Lucy Maude Montgomery's *Anne of Green Gables*, and the poetry of Walt Whitman. She took courses in creative writing at Birmingham-Southern College, before attending graduate school at the University of Iowa Writers' Workshop. Currently, she serves as Writer in Residence and Distinguished Teaching Professor at the University of Louisville; she is Program Director of the Spalding University brief-residency Master of Fine Arts in Writing. A founder and editor of *The Louisville Review* and the Fleur-de-Lis Press, she is also the author of seven books of fiction including the critically acclaimed, national bestselling *Ahab's Wife, or the Star-Gazer; Four Spirits* (a novel of the Civil Rights Movement); *Abundance, a Novel of Marie Antoinette*, and a forthcoming novel titled *Adam & Eve*. She is the recipient of the Harper Lee Award, the Southeastern Library Association Fiction Award, and fellowships from the National Endowment for the Arts, the Kentucky Arts Council, and the Kentucky Foundation for Women. Her fiction has been published in the United Kingdom and Australia, as well as translated into German, Polish, Danish, Greek, Spanish, Hebrew, Korean, and Japanese.

Jane Gentry was born in central Kentucky, on a farm in Athens. She has published two full-length collections of poetry, *A Garden in Kentucky* and *Portrait of the Artist as a White Pig*, both from Louisiana State University Press. In 2005, Press 817 in Lexington brought out her chapbook, *A Year in Kentucky*. She has also published a short volume of local history, *Looking Back at Athens*, with William M. Lamb. An English professor at the University of Kentucky, she has won the UK Alumni Association's Great Teacher Award, teaches in the Honors program, and is advisor to *Jar*, a student-edited literary magazine. Her poems have appeared widely in journals, including *Sewanee Review, Hollins Critic, Harvard Magazine, New Virginia Review, Southern Poetry Review*, and *The American Voice*. As a critic, she has published many reviews, essays, and interviews. Of particular interest are her essays about Mary Lee Settle, which have appeared in *Southern Literary Journal, Mississippi Quarterly*, and *Iron Mountain Review*. She has been awarded two Al Smith Fellowships from the Kentucky Arts Council, and has held fellowships at Yaddo in Saratoga Springs, New York, and at the Virginia Center for the Creative Arts.

Co-editor **Frederick Smock** chairs the English department, and directs the Creative Writing program, at Bellarmine University, where he received the 2005 Wyatt Faculty Award. He has published three books of poetry with Larkspur Press. His recent books include *Pax Intrantibus: A Meditation on the Poetry of Thomas Merton* (Broadstone Books), and *Craft-talk: On Writing Poetry* (Wind Publications).